Discovering Biblical Treasures

Understanding Titus

Using Semitic Bible Study Methods with a new foundation

Michael H. Koplitz

Sandra J. Koplitz

Table of Contents

Introduction

When a person is baptized as an infant and grows up in the church, their religious DNA assimilates different paradigms. The church has a message to give about Jesus Christ and His importance. Very few people study the theology and doctrines of the church to determine for themselves the accuracy of the church. The Proto-Orthodox church, which survived the pressures of the Roman Empire, decided to oppose any expression of Christianity that did not fit its dogma in its infancy. In addition, the Proto-Orthodox church would permanently destroy any writings that the rival Christians had developed.

The Gnostic Christians of Northern Egypt viewed the life of Jesus of Nazareth in a completely different way than the Proto-Orthodox church did. They saw the message about the Kingdom of Heaven as the vital purpose of Jesus. His birth, death, and resurrection are not mentioned in the Gnostic Gospels. However, did the Proto-Orthodox church destroy the Gnostic Gospels when they crushed said movement? The answer is yes and no. Yes, they destroyed what they got their hands on. No, because in 1948, copies of the Gnostic religious books were discovered in Alexandria, Egypt. Once these documents were translated, the world learned what the Gnostic Christians believed. It is fascinatingly different than what the Proto-Orthodox said about these followers of Christ.

Why is this understanding critical? Much research points to a different situation in the early years than what the church espouses. A lot of this information is available to anyone today. However, the Seminaries and churches will not openly discuss these other writings about Jesus and His disciples. The scholars teaching in most Seminaries have learned their lessons from the church and closed-minded mentors who refuse to look at other possibilities. This is because the Western European world took Christianity and changed it from a Near Eastern religion to Western religion.

There is a theory that Paul converted Mithras House Churches into Jesus House Churches. This is clear from the connection between the Mithras' and Christianity's rituals. For example, baptism was the initiation ritual of Mithras. Communion did not originate with Jesus. This ritual was a part of Mithras, where the followers would share his flesh (bread) and drink his blood (wine). There are many more rituals that Christianity picked up from Mithras. A good reference is "Christianity's Need for Mithras," which the author wrote.

Did Paul create the churches in the letters he sent, which comprise the New Testament, and if so, they must have been Jewish groups who became Jewish Christians? They would have continued with their Hebraic rituals and saw Jesus of Nazareth as the Messiah that the prophets of old had promised. They would have adopted many of Jesus' teachings and tried to live by them. The letters in the New Testament are written in Greek. However, most Jews in the Roman Empire did not speak Greek; instead, they spoke Aramaic and Hebrew. These congregations would not have understood a Greek letter from Paul.

Therefore, the letters in the New Testament must have been written in Aramaic and then transliterated into Greek. The same can be said for the Gospels, all of them. The church, over the centuries, decided who wrote the Gospels and their intent. The only Gospel we can assign to a writer is Luke. The other three are up in the air about who wrote them. While in Seminary, the author was taught that the entire New Testament was originally written in Koine Greek. However, that raised the question, "Did Jesus speak Greek?" The Seminary instructors says, "no, Jesus did not speak Greek." Then the New Testament, especially the Gospels, must have been written in Aramaic. After all, Jesus spoke Aramaic and Hebrew.

We know this because He was a poor *tekton* (a stonemason or carpenter) from an impoverished city named Nazareth. Being born to a Jewish family in Galilee, he would have learned the traditions of His people and trade. He would have learned to speak Aramaic, the language of the area. He would have learned Hebrew because that was the language of the synagogue and the Temple in Jerusalem. In other words, Hebrew was the language of God, and Jewish males learned the language.

Suppose you are ready to toss this manuscript into the nearest trash can or delete it off your electronic device at this point in the introduction. In that case, the writer has your attention. This is the reaction when the writer has spoken with persons who had been indoctrinated into the church's position since birth. The author did not come into the church environment until he was 35. Therefore, the church's paradigms, dogma, and doctrine were not a part of his DNA. Instead, he questioned a lot. He found many inconsistencies between the Bible and the doctrines of the church. Seminary was an experience to learn what the church had evolved into two-thousand years after the death of Jesus.

There are more parts to the premise that the New Testament was originally written in Aramaic and will be explored. For the reader to grasp the subsequent phases of the proof, an open mind is critical.

Culture and Language

Let us continue in the journey of examining the New Testament to determine its original language. Nothing in stone tells us that Aramaic is the Original Language of the New Testament. However, nothing says that Koine Greek was the original language of the New Testament either. Therefore, we have two theories about the original language of the New Testament. The author admits that the Seminary he attended drove home the belief that the Old Testament was written in Hebrew, except for a few spots. The New Testament was initially written in Koine Greek.

The writers' research has been searching for the original meaning of Scripture for many years. The methodology for this work is called "Ancient Bible Study Methods." The method was developed by Dr. Anne Davis of the Bible Learning University in Albuquerque, New Mexico. The author studied this method with Dr. Davis as his mentor. It became clear that the search for the original meaning of the Scriptures requires that the culture and language be examined. So, the author's methodology is Dr. Davis' work, plus his Ph.D. studies combining the method, culture, and language.

The language examination is easy for the Old Testament because it was written in Hebrew, and about one-half of Daniel is in Aramaic. It does not take long to realize that idioms and figures of speech in the Hebrew of the Old Testament revealed a lot about the people and situation of the day when the scrolls were written. The Targums were a valuable resource because they are the Aramaic translations the rabbis did for the people living outside of Judea. The rabbis added commentary to the Targums because they knew that some of the idioms and speech used in the Near East would not translate well into the different areas where the Jews lived.

The culture of the Near East has been essentially the same in many aspects since the days of Jesus. Many practices of Jesus' day are still in use today. The culture of the Jews of the Near East is built into the language. Often an Aramaic or Hebrew word has a deep meaning that is only fully understood by natives living in that culture. The Old Testament is filled with cultural items that do not need to be spelled out because the people knew their culture in the author's time.

Suppose the New Testament in Koine Greek is a transliteration of the Aramaic. The culture, figures of speech, and idioms will be easily identified when examining the Peshitta (the Aramaic version of the New Testament). Indeed many of the so-called difficult words of Jesus are not tricky when examined in the light of the culture of Jesus' day. An example is "faith to move a mountain," Jesus says these words to His disciples. The church determined that this meant complete faith in Jesus. From the western European Greek point of view, that makes sense. What else could it possibly mean?

"Faith to move a mountain" is an Aramaic idiomatic expression. What Jesus says to His followers when he says this is that his disciples needed to be faithful so that they could change the "government's view through their words." The governing body for Judaism resided on the top of a mountain. Jerusalem, with its Temple, was built on the top of Mount Zion, a very tall mountain. This idiom survived because the Aramaic Gospels were transliterated into Koine Greek. Numerous other examples support this position.

Suppose the culture and language idioms of Jesus' day can be found in the Koine Greek because it was transliterated. In that case, it supports the theory of the Aramaic versions being the original language of the Gospels and possibly even more.

The Aramaic Version of the New Testament

The Peshitta is the accepted Aramaic translation of the New Testament for many churches of the East. Peshitta means "simple, true, direct, and original." It is a collection of scrolls that were compiled in 150 CE. There were some revisions to the Peshitta in the fifth and sixth centuries. The Greek version of the New Testament is a transliteration of the Peshitta.[1]

For centuries, the Catholic church has used the Latin version of the Bible, the Vulgate, and still uses it. The Vulgate was developed around 350 CE by Jerome by order of the Pope at that time. Erasmus (1466 – 1536) was the person who put together the Greek New Testament for the Catholic church.

"The New Testament, brought to light in the original Greek tongue, was compiled and made available for humanity to study and learn. Although working under and deeply associated with the Roman Catholic Church, the learned scholar declared his disagreement with those who wanted to keep the Scriptures from the common people. He said, "If only the farmer would sing something from them at his plow, the weaver moves his shuttle to their tune, the traveler lighten the boredom of his journey with Scriptural stories!" Little did he know that the work he was about to produce would change the world forever. This Greek New Testament, in printed form, would become the standard of the New Testament, launching the translations of Martin Luther and

---

[1] Rocco A. Errico and George M. Lamsa, *Aramaic Light on Galatians through Hebrews: A Commentary Based on Aramaic, the Language of Jesus, and Ancient near Eastern Customs* (Smyma, GA: Noohra Foundation, 2005).

William Tyndale into the world. Thus, fulfilling his dream that all men would read the Bible for themselves in their common language. His new "study Bible" had two main parts, the Greek text, and a revised Latin edition, which was more elegant and accurate than the traditional translation of Jerome's Latin Vulgate. Erasmus prefaced this monumental work of scholarship with an exhortation to Bible study. He proclaimed that the New Testament contains the "philosophy of Christ," simple and accessible teaching with the power to transform lives."[2]

The church recognized Erasmus' Greek New Testament in 1515 CE. The church in the Near East has been using the Peshitta as the original language of the New Testament since 150 CE. If the Greek New Testament was important to the church as an original language, then why did it adopt the Vulgate in 350 CE? The church should have adopted the Greek New Testament at the beginning.

The Peshitta, translated into English, is used to examine Paul's letters. The rest of the methodology that the author developed for Ancient Bible Study Methods is the framework of this research.

---

[2] "Erasmus Greek New Testament," Insight of the King, accessed February 18, 2022, https://www.insightoftheking.com/erasmus-greek-new-testament.html.

The Messianic Tradition Change

One problem for Peter and the Disciples was that they claimed Yeshua to be the Messiah that the prophets of the Hebrew Scriptures spoke. However, Yeshua did not do what these traditions said. The main tradition was that the Messiah would destroy oppressive Romans and reinstate the Kingdom of Israel. Yeshua would then be declared the king and sit on David's throne in Jerusalem. That did not occur.

None of the messianic traditions of the day worked. So, what was the new movement going to do? They turned to the prophets and discovered Isaiah 50-53. These chapters are referred to as the Suffering Servant chapters. The Yeshua movement decided that the Suffering Servant was Yeshua. The portrayal of Yeshua's life does fit the Suffering Servant chapters. However, rabbinical interpretation then and now sees the Suffering Servant as the nation of Israel. Indeed, these chapters do describe the history of Israel. Nations have wanted to destroy the Jewish people since the time of Abraham.

The diaspora from the Babylonia Exile and the Assyrian invasions looked to squelch the Jewish people. The LORD promised that a remnant of the people would always survive. That is true throughout the 4,000-year history of the Jewish people. Many nations tried to destroy them, and the LORD intervened to ensure that a remnant of the people survived.

Paul must have been convinced in his encounter with Yeshua on the Damascus road that Yeshua was the Suffering Servant. It is clear from Paul's writings that he did believe this. For Paul, the Messiah was the Spiritual Messiah that the Kabbalah spoke. The

Kabbalah says that there will be two Messiahs. This theology is based on Zachariah 9:9. The first Messiah is Messiah ben Joseph. This Messiah was to restore the Kingdom of Heaven, a spiritual Kingdom. The second Messiah will be Messiah ben David. This Messiah was to restore the Kingdom of Israel. The Midrash from the Kabbalah did not state that the Messiah was two different souls.

The Kabbalah

There is a large amount of material in print about the Kabbalah. The Kabbalah referred to is Moses's Secret Work from Mount Sinai. Legends say Moses received three items on Mount Sinai when he met the LORD. The first is the written law. The written law is called the Torah. The second is the oral law. The oral law was put into a written form around 200 CE called the Mishnah. The third is the secret law called the Kabbalah. The secrets of the Kabbalah are based on the Torah and were written down around 200 CE. The main books of the Kabbalah are the Zohar and the Book of Creation.

Many of Yeshua's statements have Kabbalah undertones. Yeshua would have known the Kabbalah. Paul would have known the basics, at least, of the Kabbalah because of his religious education and training.

There are Kabbalistic ideas in the Gospels and Paul's letters. Kabbalistic verses will be highlighted in the chapters of the letters.

Methodology

The methodology employed is to use "Ancient Bible Study Methods" integrated with Jesus's day's customs and culture to examine the Hebrew and Christian Scriptures, thus gathering a more in-depth understanding by learning the Scriptures in the way the people of Jesus's day did.

I have titled the methodology of analyzing a passage of Scripture in a Hebraic manner the "Process of Discovery." The author developed this methodology, which combines various linguistic and cultural understanding areas. There are several sections to the process, and not all the parts apply to every passage of Scripture. The overall result of developing this process is to give the reader a framework for studying the Word in more depth.

The "Process of Discovery" starts with a Scripture passage. An examination of the linguistic structure of the passage is next. The linguistic structure includes parallelism, chiastic structures, and repetition. Formatting the passage in its linguistic form allows the reader to visualize what the first-century CE listener was hearing. Their corresponding sections label the chiasms, for example, A, B, C, B', A.' Not all passages of the Scriptures have a poetic form.

The next step is to "question the narrative." The narrative process of questioning the narrative assumes the reader knows nothing about the passage. Therefore, the questions go from simple to complex. The next task is to identify any linguistic patterns. Linguistic patterns include, but are not limited to, irony, simile, metaphor, symbolism, idioms, hyperbole, figurative language, personification, and allegory.

A review of any translation inconsistencies discovered between the English NAU version and Hebrew or Greek versions is done. Sometimes, a Hebrew or Greek word is translated in more than one way. Inconsistencies also can be created by the translation committee, which may have decided to use traditional language instead of the actual translation. The decision of the translation committee is in the Preface or Introduction to the Bible. Perhaps some of the inconsistencies were intentionally added to convey some deeper meaning. An examination of every discrepancy is done.

The passage is analyzed for any echoes of the Hebrew Scriptures in the Christian Scriptures. An echo occurs using a passage from the Hebrew Scriptures in the Christian Scriptures.[3] Also, echoes are found when Torah (Genesis through Deuteronomy) passages are used in other Hebrew Bible books. Cross-references in the Scripture are references from one verse to another verse, which can help the reader understand the verse.

The names of persons mentioned in the passage are listed. Many Hebrew names have meaning and may be associated with places or actions. Jewish parents used to name their children based on what they felt God had in store for their children. An example is Abraham, whose original name was Abram and was changed to mean eternal father (God changed Abram's name to Abraham, indicating a function he was to perform). When the Hebrew Bible gives names, many occurrences mean something unique. The same importance can occur for the names of places. The time it takes to travel between locations can supply insight into the event.

---

[3] Mitzvot are the 613 commandments found in the Torah that please God. There are positive and negative commandments. The list was first development by Maimonides. The full list can be found at: ttp://www.jewfaq.org/613.htm.

Keyphrases are identified in verses when they are essential to understanding that passage. There are no rules for selecting the keywords. Searching for other occurrences of the keywords in Scripture in concordance is necessary to understand the Word's usage; this must be done in either Hebrew or Greek, not in English. A classic Hebraic approach is to find the usage of a word in the Scripture by finding other verses that contain the Word. The usage of a word in its original language is discovered by searching the Scripture in the language of the Word. Verses that contain the Word are identified, and a pattern for the usage of the Word is discovered. Each verse is examined to see what the usage of the Word is, which may reveal a model for the Word's usage. The first usage of the Word in the Scripture, primarily if used in the Torah, is essential for Hebrew words. The Christian Scriptures are used for Greek words to determine the Word usage in the Scripture. Sometimes, finding the equivalent Greek Word in the Septuagint can be beneficial as analyzing its Hebrew usage.

The Rules of Hillel are used when applicable. Hillel was a Torah scholar who lived shortly before Jesus' day. Hillel developed several rules for Torah students to interpret the Scriptures, which refer to halachic Midrash. In several cases, these rules are helpful in the analysis of the Scripture.

The cultural implications from the writing period are done after the linguistic analysis is completed. The culture is crucial because it is not explicitly referenced in the biblical narratives, as indicated earlier.

From the linguistic analysis and the cultural understanding, it is possible to obtain a deeper meaning of the Scripture beyond the plain text's literal meaning. That is what the listeners of Jesus's time were doing. They put linguistics and culture together without even having to contemplate it.

The analysis will lead to findings explaining the passage's meaning in Jesus's day. Most of the time, the Hebraic analysis leads to the desire for more in-depth analysis to fully understand what Jesus was talking about or what was happening to Him. Whatever the result, a new, more in-depth understanding of the Scripture is obtained.

The components of the Process of Discovery are:

Language

Process of Discovery

Linguistics Section

Linguistic Structure

Discussion

Questioning the Passage

Verse Comparison of citations or proof text

Translation Inconsistencies

Biblical Personalities

Biblical Locations

Phrase Study

Linguistic Echoes

Rules of Hillel

Culture Section

Discussion

Questioning the passage

Cultural Echoes

Culture and Linguistics Section

Discussion

Thoughts

Only the applicable sections are included in this document.

Introduction to the Epistle

Scholars debate this Pauline epistle whether Paul wrote the letter is not. Paul wrote the epistle from Nicopolis of Macedonia before his imprisonment. People knew Titus as a Syrian and one of Paul's earliest disciples. He went with Paul on several of his missionary journeys. Titus seems to have been a brilliant organizer and administrator. He knew and understood the lives of the people in Asia Minor and Macedonia. During their years together, Paul sent Titus out on several solo journeys. Paul and Titus went to Crete. Paul left Titus behind in Crete to organize the churches and appoint elders over the congregations. In this letter, Paul sets forth the qualifications for elders. The usual warnings against any other forms of Christianity is repeated.

Chapter One

Language

Peshitta	New American Standard 1995
Titus 1:1 Paul, a servant of God, and a legate of Jesus the Messiah; according to the faith of the elect of God, and the knowledge of the truth which is in the fear of God, **2** concerning the hope of eternal life, which the veracious God promised before the times of the world; **3** and in due time he hath manifested his word, by means of our announcement, which was confided to me by the command of God our Life-giver; **4** to Titus, a real son after the common faith: Grace and peace from God our Father, and from our Lord Jesus the Messiah, our Life-giver. **5** For this cause left I thee in Crete, that thou mightest regulate the things deficient, and establish elders in every city, as I directed thee: **6** him who is blameless, who is the husband of one wife, and hath believing children, who are no revellers, nor ungovernable in sensuality. **7** For an elder ought to be blameless, as the steward of God; and not be self-willed, nor irascible, nor excessive in wine, nor with hands swift to strike, nor a lover of base gains. **8** But he should be a lover of strangers, and a lover of good [deeds], and be sober, upright, kind-hearted, and restraining himself from evil passions; **9** and studious of the doctrine of the word of faith, that he may be able by his wholesome teaching both to	**Titus 1:1** Paul, [a]a bond-servant of God and an [b]apostle of Jesus Christ, [1]for the faith of those [c]chosen of God and [d]the knowledge of the truth which is [e]according to godliness, **2** in [a]the hope of eternal life, which God, [b]who cannot lie, [c]promised [1d]long ages ago, **3** but [a]at the proper time manifested, *even* His word, in [b]the proclamation [c]with which I was entrusted [d]according to the commandment of [e]God our Savior, **Titus 1:4** To [a]Titus, [b]my true child [1]in a [c]common faith: [d]Grace and peace from God the Father and [e]Christ Jesus our Savior. **Titus 1:5** For this reason I left you in [a]Crete, that you would set in order what remains and [b]appoint [c]elders in every city as I directed you, **6** *namely,* [a]if any man is above reproach, the [b]husband of one wife, having children who believe, not accused of [c]dissipation or [d]rebellion. **7** For the [1a]overseer must be above reproach as [b]God's steward, not [c]self-willed, not quick-tempered, not [d]addicted to wine, not pugnacious, [e]not fond of sordid gain, **8** but [a]hospitable, [b]loving what is good, sensible, just, devout, self-controlled, **9** [a]holding fast the faithful word which is in accordance with the teaching, so that he will be able both to exhort in [b]sound

console, and to rebuke them that are contentious. **10** For many are unsubmissive, and their discourses vain; and they mislead the minds of people, especially such as are of the circumcision. **11** The mouth of these ought to be stopped: they corrupt many families; and they teach what they ought not, for the sake of base gains. **12** One of them, a prophet of their own, said, The Cretans are always mendacious, evil beasts, idle bellies. **13** And this testimony is true. Therefore chide them sharply; that they may be sound in the faith, **14** and may not throw themselves into Jewish fables, and into the precepts of men who hate the truth. **15** For to the pure, every thing is pure; but to them who are defiled and unbelieving, nothing is pure; but their understanding is defiled, and their conscience. **16** And they profess that they know God, but in their works they deny him; and they are odious, and disobedient, and to every good work reprobates.

doctrine and to refute those who contradict.

Titus 1:10 *a*For there are many *b*rebellious men, *c*empty talkers and deceivers, especially *d*those of the circumcision, **11** who must be silenced because they are upsetting *a*whole families, teaching *b*things they should not *teach* *c*for the sake of sordid gain. **12** One of themselves, a prophet of their own, says, "*a*Cretans are always liars, evil beasts, lazy gluttons." **13** This testimony is true. For this reason *a*reprove them *b*severely so that they may be *c*sound in the faith, **14** not paying attention to Jewish *a*myths and *b*commandments of men who *c*turn away from the truth. **15** *a*To the pure, all things are pure; but *b*to those who are defiled and unbelieving, nothing is pure, but both their *c*mind and their conscience are defiled. **16** *a*They profess to know God, but by *their* deeds they *b*deny *Him,* being *c*detestable and *d*disobedient and *e*worthless *f*for any good deed.

References to the New American Standard 1995

Titus 1:1

[1]Or *according to*
[a]Rom 1:1; James 1:1; Rev 1:1
[b]2 Cor 1:1
[c]Luke 18:7
[d]1 Tim 2:4
[e]1 Tim 6:3

Titus 1:2

[1]Lit *before times eternal*
[a]2 Tim 1:1; Titus 3:7
[b]2 Tim 2:13; Heb 6:18
[c]Rom 1:2
[d]2 Tim 1:9

Titus 1:3

[a]1 Tim 2:6
[b]Rom 16:25; 2 Tim 4:17
[c]1 Tim 1:11
[d]1 Tim 1:1
[e]Luke 1:47; 1 Tim 1:1; Titus 2:10; 3:4

Titus 1:4

[1]Lit *according to*
[a]2 Cor 2:13; 8:23; Gal 2:3; 2 Tim 4:10
[b]2 Tim 1:2
[c]2 Pet 1:1
[d]Rom 1:7
[e]1 Tim 1:12; 2 Tim 1:1

Titus 1:5

[a]Acts 27:7; Titus 1:12
[b]Acts 14:23
[c]Acts 11:30

Titus 1:6

[a]1 Tim 3:2-4; Titus 1:6-8

[b]1 Tim 3:2
[c]Eph 5:18
[d]Titus 1:10

Titus 1:7
[1]Or *bishop*
[a]1 Tim 3:2
[b]1 Cor 4:1
[c]2 Pet 2:10
[d]1 Tim 3:3
[e]1 Tim 3:3, 8

Titus 1:8
[a]1 Tim 3:2
[b]2 Tim 3:3

Titus 1:9
[a]2 Thess 2:15; 1 Tim 1:19; 2 Tim 1:13
[b]1 Tim 1:10; Titus 2:1

Titus 1:10
[a]2 Cor 11:13
[b]Titus 1:6
[c]1 Tim 1:6
[d]Acts 11:2

Titus 1:11
[a]1 Tim 5:4; 2 Tim 3:6
[b]1 Tim 5:13
[c]1 Tim 6:5

Titus 1:12
[a]Acts 2:11; 27:7

Titus 1:13
[a]1 Tim 5:20; 2 Tim 4:2; Titus 2:15
[b]2 Cor 13:10
[c]Titus 2:2

Titus 1:14
[a]1 Tim 1:4

[b]Col 2:22
[c]2 Tim 4:4

Titus 1:15

[a]Luke 11:41; Rom 14:20
[b]Rom 14:14, 23
[c]1 Tim 6:5

Titus 1:16

[a]1 John 2:4
[b]1 Tim 5:8
[c]Rev 21:8
[d]Titus 3:3
[e]2 Tim 3:8
[f]2 Tim 3:17; Titus 3:1

Koine Greek

Titus 1:1   Παυλος δουλος θεου, αποστολος δε Ιησου Χριστου κατα πιστιν εκλεκτων θεου και επιγνωσιν αληθειας της κατ' ευσεβειαν [2] επ' ελπιδι ζωης αιωνιου, ην επηγγειλατο ο αψευδης θεος προ χρονων αιωνιων, [3] εφανερωσεν δε καιροις ιδιοις τον λογον αυτου εν κηρυγματι, ο επιστευθην εγω κατ' επιταγην του σωτηρος ημων θεου, [4] Τιτω γνησιω τεκνω κατα κοινην πιστιν, χαρις και ειρηνη απο θεου πατρος και Χριστου Ιησου του σωτηρος ημων.

Titus 1:5   Τουτου χαριν απελιπον σε εν Κρητη, ινα τα λειποντα επιδιορθωση και καταστησης κατα πολιν πρεσβυτερους, ως εγω σοι διεταξαμην, [6] ει τις εστιν ανεγκλητος, μιας γυναικος ανηρ, τεκνα εχων πιστα, μη εν κατηγορια ασωτιας η ανυποτακτα. [7] δει γαρ τον επισκοπον ανεγκλητον ειναι ως θεου οικονομον, μη αυθαδη, μη οργιλον, μη παροινον, μη πληκτην, μη αισχροκερδη, [8] αλλα φιλοξενον φιλαγαθον σωφρονα δικαιον οσιον εγκρατη, [9] αντεχομενον του κατα την διδαχην πιστου λογου, ινα δυνατος η και παρακαλειν εν τη διδασκαλια τη υγιαινουση και τους αντιλεγοντας ελεγχειν.

Titus 1:10   Εισιν γαρ πολλοι και ανυποτακτοι, ματαιολογοι και φρεναπαται, μαλιστα οι εκ της περιτομης, [11] ους δει επιστομιζειν, οιτινες ολους οικους ανατρεπουσιν διδασκοντες α μη δει αισχρου κερδους χαριν. [12] ειπεν τις εξ αυτων ιδιος αυτων προφητης·
Κρητες αει ψευσται, κακα θηρια, γαστερες αργαι.

Titus 1:13   η μαρτυρια αυτη εστιν αληθης. δι' ην αιτιαν ελεγχε αυτους αποτομως, ινα υγιαινωσιν εν τη πιστει, [14] μη προσεχοντες Ιουδαικοις μυθοις και εντολαις ανθρωπων αποστρεφομενων την αληθειαν. [15] παντα καθαρα τοις καθαροις· τοις δε μεμιαμμενοις και απιστοις ουδεν καθαρον, αλλα μεμιανται αυτων και ο νους και η συνειδησις. [16] θεον ομολογουσιν ειδεναι, τοις δε εργοις αρνουνται, βδελυκτοι οντες και απειθεις και προς παν εργον αγαθον αδοκιμοι.

Language

  Process of Discovery

    Linguistics Section

    Linguistic Structure

[Introducing himself] 1 Paul, [a]a bond-servant of God and an [b]apostle of Jesus Christ, [1]for the faith of those [c]chosen of God and [d]the knowledge of the truth which is [e]according to godliness, **2** in [a]the hope of eternal life, which God, [b]who cannot lie, [c]promised [1d]long ages ago, **3** but [a]at the proper time manifested, *even* His word, in [b]the proclamation [c]with which I was entrusted [d]according to the commandment of [e]God our Savior,

[Greeting] 4 To [a]Titus, [b]my true child [1]in a [c]common faith: [d]Grace and peace from God the Father and [e]Christ Jesus our Savior.

[Attributes for an elder and overseer] Titus 1:5 For this reason I left you in [a]Crete, that you would set in order what remains and [b]appoint [c]elders in every city as I directed you, **6** *namely,* [a]if any man is above reproach, the [b]husband of one wife, having children who believe, not accused of [c]dissipation or [d]rebellion. **7** For the [1a]overseer must be above reproach as [b]God's steward, not [c]self-willed, not quick-tempered, not [d]addicted to wine, not pugnacious, [e]not fond of sordid gain, **8** but [a]hospitable, [b]loving what is good, sensible, just, devout, self-controlled, **9** [a]holding fast the faithful word which is in accordance with the teaching, so that he will be able both to exhort in [b]sound doctrine and to refute those who contradict.

[Silence those who oppose his definition of Christianity]10 [a]For there are many [b]rebellious men, [c]empty talkers and deceivers, especially [d]those of the circumcision, **11** who must be silenced because they are upsetting [a]whole families, teaching [b]things they should not *teach* [c]for the sake of sordid gain. **12** One of themselves, a prophet of their own, says, "[a]Cretans are always liars, evil beasts, lazy gluttons." **13** This testimony is true. For this reason [a]reprove them [b]severely so that they may be [c]sound in the faith, **14** not paying attention to Jewish [a]myths and [b]commandments of men who [c]turn away from the truth. **15** [a]To the pure, all things are pure; but [b]to those who are defiled and unbelieving, nothing is pure, but both their [c]mind and their conscience are defiled. **16** [a]They profess to know God, but by *their* deeds they [b]deny *Him,* being [c]detestable and [d]disobedient and [e]worthless [f]for any good deed.

Discussion

This is a typical introduction to the letter style of the day. As usual, Paul tells Titus that he is the only true source of the meaning of Yeshua's sacrifice.

Questioning the Passage

1. Who is the elect and who chose them? (v. 1)

    The belief was that there was a pre-chosen group of souls that were granted automatic entrance into Heaven. People referred to this group as the elect. Martin Luther and the Pope in 1519 argued back and forth about who was in the elect and who was not. If a soul was in the elect, it did not matter what they did on earth. Instantly, their sins were forgiven, and they were assured entrance into Heaven. In Paul's day, he was referring to the believers in his form of Christianity. He believed this group was chosen by God to enter heaven with forgiveness.

2. What is the knowledge of truth? (v. 1)

    The knowledge of truth, according to Paul, was his decisions on what the life of Yeshua was. Paul took a large amount of the doctrine from the Mithras cult and adopted it for his form of Christianity. There is a huge crossover between Mithras and Yeshua worship. 90% of the rituals of Paul's Christianity came from the Mithras cult.

3. How did God promise eternal life before the creation of the world? (v. 2)

    The Zohar (Jewish and Christian mysticism's key text) says that the spirit of the Torah came before the LORD when He was about to create humanity. The Torah pleaded with the LORD to not create humanity. Since the Torah was the blueprint for creation, humanity had to be created since Adam and Eve were a part of the

Torah. The LORD told the Torah not to worry about humanity. The Torah said to the LORD that humanity would sin against the Laws (mitzvot). The LORD said that He knew this and created repentance into the Torah, thus into the fabric of the Universe. Therefore, eternal life is a part of the Universe. The author is referring to the knowledge that the LORD created a way to seek and receive repentance. This was accomplished by having faith in the life-giving ways of Yeshua the Messiah.

4. Is Paul saying that he was the only person entrusted with the message of eternal life and not Yeshua? (v. 3)

Paul is saying that he received the entrusted message of salvation through our Savior, Jesus Christ. Paul is saying that he acted like a prophet when he was bringing the message of salvation to the people.

5. What was the culture of a teacher calling a student "a child?" (v. 4)

It was common and cultural for a teacher (or rabbi) to refer to his students as his children. The teacher would do whatever he could to teach and take care of his students (his disciples).

6. How old was Titus when this letter was written? (v. 4)

The exact age of Titus, as referenced in the Bible, is not specified. However, based on the context provided in the New Testament, we can infer that he was likely an adult during his interactions with the Apostle Paul. Since there are no specific details about his age at the time of his involvement in Paul's ministry, we cannot determine it with certainty from the biblical text alone.

7. Did Paul visit all the cities of Crete? (v. 5)

The verse infers that Paul visited Crete with Titus. He indicated he left Titus there. This is the only reference in the New Testament to Paul and Crete.

8. How did Titus determine who could be an elder? (v. 5)

Verses six through nine define who could be an elder.

9. Did Paul say that an elder is an overseer? (v. 7)

The elder was a person who exercised leadership within a specific house church. The overseer (or bishop) was to exercise leadership over the elders of the local churches. Such a hierarchy did not exist then or now in Judaism. Synagogues are loosely connected by an association group. Therefore, one rabbi cannot tell another rabbi how to lead his congregation. Therefore, the idea of a hierarchy must have come from the Mithras Cult since Paul converted these house churches into Yeshua house churches.

10. Who are "those of the circumcision?" (v. 11)

This is the author's way of referring to the Jewish people in Crete.

11. How did Paul define whole families? (v. 11)

Paul's definition of family is primarily based on his teachings in the New Testament, especially in his letters to various early Christian communities. In Paul's writings, he often used the concept of family to describe the relationships within the Christian community and the broader understanding of familial bonds among believers. Here are some key aspects of Paul's view on family:

Paul frequently refers to fellow believers as brothers and sisters, emphasizing the spiritual bond and unity that Christians share in Christ. He uses terms like "brothers," "sisters," and "children" to describe the relationships within the Christian community.

Paul emphasizes the importance of love and unity within the Christian family. In Galatians 6:10, he writes, "So then, as we have opportunity, let us do good to everyone, and especially to those who are of the household of faith. This emphasizes the concept of the Christian community as a caring and supportive family.

Paul also addresses specific roles and responsibilities within the family and the broader church community. For example, in Ephesians 5:22-6:4, he discusses the roles of husbands and wives, parents and children, and masters and slaves, emphasizing mutual respect, submission, and love.

Paul's teachings on family also reflect a sense of inclusion and equality. In Galatians 3:28, he states, "There is neither Jew nor Greek, there is neither slave nor free, there is no male and female, for you are all one in Christ Jesus." This highlights the idea that in Christ, all believers are part of the same family regardless of social status, ethnicity, or gender.

Overall, Paul's understanding of family in the Christian context emphasizes spiritual kinship, love, unity, mutual support, and fulfilling roles and responsibilities within the community of believers.

12. What was the sordid gain? (v. 11)

"Sordid gain" refers to money or profit obtained in a dishonest, immoral, or dishonorable way. In religious and ethical contexts, the term is often used to condemn or criticize financial gain that come from exploiting others, engaging in corruption, or participating in activities that are considered morally reprehensible. It can encompass various forms of unethical behavior, such as fraud, exploitation, bribery, or deceitful practices aimed at personal enrichment at the expense of others or the common good.

13. Who is the prophet from Crete? (v. 12)

In Titus 1:12, the prophet from Crete, referred to by Paul is Epimenides. Paul quotes a line from Epimenides in this verse, which says, "Cretans are always liars, evil beasts, lazy gluttons." Paul uses this quotation to illustrate a point about the character of certain people in Crete, highlighting a cultural stereotype of the time.

14. Was there religious tolerance according to Paul? (v. 13-16)

In Titus 1:13-16, Paul addresses issues related to religious tolerance and the conduct of certain individuals within the community. Here's a breakdown of those verses:

Titus 1:13-14: Paul criticizes certain individuals, likely referring to false teachers or those causing division within the church. He instructs Titus to rebuke them sharply, so they may be sound in the faith and not give heed to Jewish myths or commandments of men who turn away from the truth.

In Titus 1:15, Paul then makes a broader statement about purity and defilement, saying, "Those who are pure consider all things pure." This can be understood as a statement about the spiritual state of individuals affecting their perception of purity or impurity.

Titus 1:16: In this verse, Paul describes the behavior of those who profess to know God but deny Him by their works. He lists various negative attributes, such as being detestable, disobedient, and unfit for any good work. This may imply that religious tolerance, in Paul's view, does not extend to those whose actions contradict their profession of faith.

Overall, while Paul does not directly address religious tolerance in the specific sense of accepting diverse religious beliefs or practices, his emphasis on sound doctrine, truth, and the behavior consistent with one's faith suggests that there were boundaries to tolerance for those who opposed or undermined the core teachings of Christianity.

Biblical Personalities

1. Titus - Titus, in the New Testament, was a companion and co-worker of the apostle Paul. He appears in several of Paul's letters and is mentioned in the Book of Acts. Titus is believed to have been a Gentile convert to Christianity and was closely associated with Paul's missionary work.

Titus is mentioned in the following New Testament books:

- Galatians: Titus accompanied Paul and Barnabas to Jerusalem during the controversy over circumcision.
- 2 Corinthians: Titus is mentioned as Paul's partner in ministry and as the bearer of Paul's severe letter to the Corinthians.

- 2 Corinthians: Paul speaks highly of Titus, describing him as his brother and fellow worker.

- 2 Corinthians: Titus is praised for his eagerness and zeal in serving the Corinthian church.

- 2 Corinthians: Paul indicates that Titus is bringing news from Corinth to Paul in Macedonia.

- 2 Corinthians: Paul expresses his gratitude to God for the comfort he received through Titus.

- 2 Corinthians: Paul mentions that Titus would be returning to Corinth with another brother to collect a collection for the saints.

- 2 Corinthians: Titus is described as Paul's partner and fellow worker in writing to the Corinthian church.

- 2 Corinthians: Paul instructs the Corinthians to welcome Titus with joy and respect.

From these references, it's clear that Titus played a significant role in Paul's ministry and in the early Christian community.

Biblical Locations

1. Crete

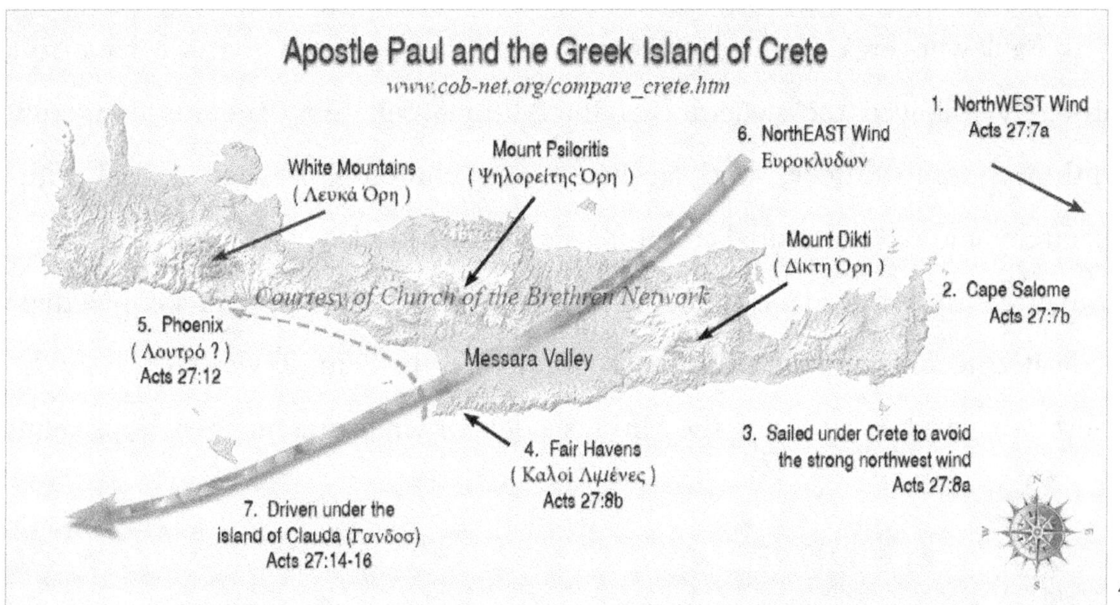

Culture Section

Discussion

Titus was called an overseer, which in today's language would be a bishop. The term "Elders" means presbyters or ministers. They were called elders because Semitic people rarely ordained young men to the ministry. They preferred older men who had experienced good, moral conduct, and reputation.

In the Near East, it is the behavior of a priest that counts and not the quality of his sermons.

---

4 1. Ronald J. Gordon, Apostle Paul and the winds of crete, February 18, 2016, https://cob-net.org/compare_crete.php.

Thoughts

It is Paul who created the hierarchy inside of the church that we have today. It probably followed the structure of the Mithras cult. As Paul was converting the Mithras house churches into Yeshua house churches, he had a deal with their hierarchy and organizational structure. Paul left it in place but removed many of the converted Mithras elders and overseers and replace them with people that were dedicated to his form of Christianity. Paul used his Semitic views on how an elder must behave when replacing the Mithras elders or when creating new house churches.

Chapter Two

Language

Peshitta	New American Standard 1995
Titus 2:1 But speak thou the things that belong to wholesome doctrine. **2** And teach the older men to be watchful in their minds, and to be sober, and to be pure, and to be sound in the faith, and in love and in patience. **3** And so also the elder women, that they be in behavior as becometh the fear of God; and not to be slanderers; and not to be addicted to much wine; and to be inculcators of good things, **4** making the younger women to be modest, to love their husbands and their children, **5** to be chaste and holy, and to take good care of their households, and to be obedient to their husbands; so that no one may reproach the word of God. **6** And likewise exhort young men to be sober. **7** And in every thing show thyself a pattern, as to all good works: and in thy teaching, let thy discourse be healthful, **8** such as is sober and uncorrupt; and let no one despise it: so that he who riseth up against us, may be ashamed, seeing he can say nothing odious against us. **9** Let servants obey their masters in every thing, and strive to please them, and not contradict, nor pilfer; **10** but let them manifest that their fidelity, in all respects, is good: so that they may adorn the doctrine of God our Life-giver, in all things. **11** For the all-vivifying grace of God, is revealed to all	**Titus 2:1** But as for you, speak the things which are fitting for [a]sound doctrine. **2** [a]Older men are to be [b]temperate, dignified, sensible, [c]sound [d]in faith, in love, in [1]perseverance. **Titus 2:3** Older women likewise are to be reverent in their behavior, [a]not malicious gossips nor [b]enslaved to much wine, teaching what is good, **4** so that they may [1]encourage the young women to love their husbands, to love their children, **5** *to be* sensible, pure, [a]workers at home, kind, being [b]subject to their own husbands, [c]so that the word of God will not be dishonored. **Titus 2:6** Likewise urge [a]the young men to be [1]sensible; **7** in all things show yourself to be [a]an example of good deeds, *with* [1]purity in doctrine, dignified, **8** sound *in* speech which is beyond reproach, so [a]that the opponent will be put to shame, having nothing bad to say about us. **Titus 2:9** *Urge* [a]bondslaves to be subject to their own masters in everything, to be well-pleasing, not [1]argumentative, **10** not pilfering, but showing all good faith so that they will adorn the doctrine of [a]God our Savior in every respect. **Titus 2:11** For the grace of God has [a]appeared, [1b]bringing salvation to all men,

men; **12** and it teacheth us, to deny ungodliness and worldly lusts, and to live in this world in sobriety, and in uprightness, and in the fear of God, **13** looking for the blessed hope, and the manifestation of the glory of the great God, and our Life-giver, Jesus the Messiah; **14** who gave himself for us, that he might recover us from all iniquity, and purify for himself a new people, who are zealous in good works. **15** These things speak thou, and exhort, and inculcate, with all authority; and let no one despise thee.

12 [1]instructing us to deny ungodliness and [a]worldly desires and [b]to live sensibly, righteously and godly [c]in the present age, **13** looking for the blessed hope and the [a]appearing of the glory of [1b]our great God and Savior, Christ Jesus, **14** who [a]gave Himself for us [b]to redeem us from every lawless deed, and to [c]purify for Himself a [d]people for His own possession, [e]zealous for good deeds.

Titus 2:15 These things speak and [a]exhort and [a]reprove with all [1]authority. [b]Let no one disregard you.

References to the New American Standard 1995

Titus 2:1
[a]Titus 1:9

Titus 2:2
[1]Or *steadfastness*
[a]Philem 9
[b]1 Tim 3:2
[c]Titus 1:13
[d]1 Tim 1:2, 14

Titus 2:3
[a]1 Tim 3:11
[b]1 Tim 3:8

Titus 2:4
[1]Or *train*

Titus 2:5
[a]1 Tim 5:14
[b]Eph 5:22
[c]1 Tim 6:1

Titus 2:6
[1]Or *sensible in all things; show*
[a]1 Tim 5:1

Titus 2:7
[1]Or *soundness;* lit *uncorruptness*
[a]1 Tim 4:12

Titus 2:8
[a]2 Thess 3:14; 1 Pet 2:12

Titus 2:9
[1]Lit *contradicting*
[a]Eph 6:5; 1 Tim 6:1

Titus 2:10
[a]Titus 1:3

Titus 2:11
[1]Or *to all men, bringing*
[a]2 Tim 1:10; Titus 3:4
[b]1 Tim 2:4

Titus 2:12
[1]Or *disciplining*
[a]1 Tim 6:9; Titus 3:3
[b]2 Tim 3:12
[c]1 Tim 6:17

Titus 2:13
[1]Or *the great God and our Savior*
[a]2 Thess 2:8
[b]1 Tim 1:1; 2 Tim 1:2; Titus 1:4; 2 Pet 1:1

Titus 2:14
[a]1 Tim 2:6
[b]Ps 130:8; 1 Pet 1:18f
[c]Ezek 37:23; Heb 1:3; 9:14; 1 John 1:7
[d]Ex 19:5; Deut 4:20; 7:6; 14:2; Eph 1:11; 1 Pet 2:9
[e]Eph 2:10; Titus 3:8; 1 Pet 3:13

Titus 2:15
[1]Lit *command*
[a]1 Tim 4:13; 5:20; 2 Tim 4:2
[b]1 Tim 4:12

Koine Greek

Titus 2:1   Συ δε λαλει α πρεπει τη υγιαινουση διδασκαλια. ² Πρεσβυτας νηφαλιους ειναι, σεμνους, σωφρονας, υγιαινοντας τη πιστει, τη αγαπη, τη υπομονη· ³ πρεσβυτιδας ωσαυτως εν καταστηματι ιεροπρεπεις, μη διαβολους μη οινω πολλω δεδουλωμενας, καλοδιδασκαλους, ⁴ ινα σωφρονιζωσιν τας νεας φιλανδρους ειναι, φιλοτεκνους ⁵ σωφρονας αγνας οικουργους αγαθας, υποτασσομενας τοις ιδιοις ανδρασιν, ινα μη ο λογος του θεου βλασφημηται.

Titus 2:6   Τους νεωτερους ωσαυτως παρακαλει σωφρονειν ⁷ περι παντα, σεαυτον παρεχομενος τυπον καλων εργων, εν τη διδασκαλια αφθοριαν, σεμνοτητα, ⁸ λογον υγιη ακαταγνωστον, ινα ο εξ εναντιας εντραπη μηδεν εχων λεγειν περι ημων φαυλον.

Titus 2:9   Δουλους ιδιοις δεσποταις υποτασσεσθαι εν πασιν, ευαρεστους ειναι, μη αντιλεγοντας, ¹⁰ μη νοσφιζομενους, αλλα πασαν πιστιν ενδεικνυμενους αγαθην, ινα την διδασκαλιαν την του σωτηρος ημων θεου κοσμωσιν εν πασιν.

Titus 2:11   Επεφανη γαρ η χαρις του θεου σωτηριος πασιν ανθρωποις ¹² παιδευουσα ημας, ινα αρνησαμενοι την ασεβειαν και τας κοσμικας επιθυμιας σωφρονως και δικαιως και ευσεβως ζησωμεν εν τω νυν αιωνι, ¹³ προσδεχομενοι την μακαριαν ελπιδα και επιφανειαν της δοξης του μεγαλου θεου και σωτηρος ημων Ιησου Χριστου, ¹⁴ ος εδωκεν εαυτον υπερ ημων, ινα λυτρωσηται ημας απο πασης ανομιας και καθαριση εαυτω λαον περιουσιον, ζηλωτην καλων εργων. ¹⁵ Ταυτα λαλει και παρακαλει και ελεγχε μετα πασης επιταγης· μηδεις σου περιφρονειτω.

Language

  Process of Discovery

    Linguistics Section

      Linguistic Structure

[Duties for older men] Titus 2:1 But as for you, speak the things which are fitting for *a*sound doctrine. **2** *a*Older men are to be *b*temperate, dignified, sensible, *c*sound *d*in faith, in love, in [1]perseverance.

[Duties for older women] Titus 2:3 Older women likewise are to be reverent in their behavior, *a*not malicious gossips nor *b*enslaved to much wine, teaching what is good, **4** so that they may [1]encourage the young women to love their husbands, to love their children, **5** *to be* sensible, pure, *a*workers at home, kind, being *b*subject to their own husbands, *c*so that the word of God will not be dishonored.

[Duties of younger men] Titus 2:6 Likewise urge *a*the young men to be [1]sensible; **7** in all things show yourself to be *a*an example of good deeds, *with* [1]purity in doctrine, dignified, **8** sound *in* speech which is beyond reproach, so *a*that the opponent will be put to shame, having nothing bad to say about us.

[Duties of bondslaves] Titus 2:9 *Urge* *a*bondslaves to be subject to their own masters in everything, to be well-pleasing, not [1]argumentative, **10** not pilfering, but showing all good faith so that they will adorn the doctrine of *a*God our Savior in every respect.

[Benediction] Titus 2:11 For the grace of God has *a*appeared, [1b]bringing salvation to all men, **12** [1]instructing us to deny ungodliness and *a*worldly desires and *b*to live sensibly, righteously and godly *c*in the present age, **13** looking for the blessed hope and the *a*appearing of the glory of [1b]our great God and Savior, Christ Jesus, **14** who *a*gave Himself for us *b*to redeem us from every lawless deed, and to *c*purify for Himself a *d*people for His own possession, *e*zealous for good deeds. **15** These things speak and *a*exhort and *a*reprove with all [1]authority. *b*Let no one disregard you.

Discussion

This chapter outlines the duties and behaviors of people who have authority in the church.

Questioning the Passage

1. What is sound doctrine? (v. 1)

When Paul referred to "sound doctrine" in his letters, he was emphasizing the importance of healthy teaching for the well-being of Christians and the church.[5]

The term "sound" translates to "healthy" and this healthy or sound doctrine is a pattern that, when followed, promotes healthy faith and love[1]. It is not just about intellectual understanding or theological concepts, but it has also been about how those teachings shape our lives and relationships.[6]

In his letter to Titus, for example, Paul clarified that 'sound doctrine' or 'healthy teaching' is primarily a matter of living out moral character and being consistent in their lifestyles.

Sound doctrine is considered a valuable heritage that should be treasured in this generation and faithfully transmitted to the next. It has about the teachings from God, about God that direct us to the glory of God. So sound doctrine is about

---

[5] 1. "What Is Sound Doctrine?," Ligonier Ministries, accessed April 15, 2024, https://www.ligonier.org/learn/articles/what-sound-doctrine.

[6] 1. Paul VargasPaul Vargas 3 et al., "What Does Paul Mean by 'Sound Doctrine' in Titus 2:1," Biblical Hermeneutics Stack Exchange, January 1, 1960, https://hermeneutics.stackexchange.com/questions/8649/what-does-paul-mean-by-sound-doctrine-in-titus-21.

understanding God's teachings and applying them in a way that leads to a healthy and loving faith.[7]

2. What does "subject to their husbands" mean? (v. 5)

The phrase "subject to their husbands" in Titus 2:5 refers to the idea of wives being supportive and respectful towards their husbands within the context of a Christian marriage. It is part of a larger passage where Paul is instructing how various groups in the church should conduct themselves to reflect Christian values.

3. What is purity in doctrine? (v. 7)

Purity and doctrine mean that the person is following Paul's form of Christianity to the letter.

4. Who is the opponent of doctrine? (v. 8)

They considered anyone who did not believe in exactly what Paul said about Christianity and the worship of God through Yeshua to be an opponent of doctrine. There was competition in the ancient world which form of Christianity would survive. The biggest threat Paul faced was the Gnostics from Northern Egypt. There were the Jewish Christians coming from Jerusalem who saw Christianity in a completely different light than Paul did. Today, this is called Semitic Christianity.

5. What is ungodliness? (v. 12)

Ungodliness refers to the quality or state of being ungodly. To be ungodly is to act in a way that is contrary to the nature of God, to actively oppose God in disobedience, or to have an irreverent disregard for God. Ungodliness is the

---

[7] 1. Posted by Marsha West and Marsha West, "What Is Sound Doctrine?," Christian Research Network, February 15, 2017, https://christianresearchnetwork.org/2017/02/15/what-is-sound-doctrine/.

condition of being polluted with sin. It can also refer to not accepting God or a particular religious doctrine. Ungodliness is a state or behavior that is contrary to the teachings and values of God.[8]

6. How did one live godly in the ancient world of Paul? (v. 12)

The way to live godly in the ancient world of Paul was to learn the mitzvot of the Torah and live by them using Yeshua as the example.

Thoughts

It is important to live in a way that God would prefer. The best way to do this is through the example of Yeshua in the Gospels. Yeshua fulfilled the Torah and the prophets, demonstrating the right way to live according to God's laws. During his time, the religious leaders were attempting to persuade people to follow God's law according to their own preferences. Sometimes that works well and at other times it becomes more of a burden. Yeshua freed us from interpreting those who did not fully understand the Scriptures.

---

[8] 1. GotQuestions.org, "Home," GotQuestions.org, April 26, 2016, https://www.gotquestions.org/ungodly-ungodliness.html.

Chapter Three

Language

Peshitta	New American Standard 1995
Titus 3:1 And admonish them to be submissive and obedient to princes and potentates; and that they be ready for every good work; **2** and that they speak ill of no man; that they be not contentious, but mild; and that in every thing they manifest benignity towards all men. **3** For we also were formerly reckless, and disobedient, and erring, and serving divers lusts, and living in malice and envy, and were hateful and also hating one another. **4** But when the kindness and compassion of God our Life-giver was revealed, **5** not by works of righteousness which we had done, but according to his mercy, he vivified us, by the washing of the new birth, and by the renovation of the Holy Spirit, **6** which he shed on us abundantly, by Jesus the Messiah our Life-giver: **7** that we might be justified by his grace, and become heirs in the hope of eternal life. **8** Faithful is the word: and in these things, I would have thee also establish them; so that they, who have believed in God, may be careful to cultivate good works: these are the things, which are good, and profitable to men. **9** But foolish questions, and stories of genealogies, and the disputes and contests of the scribes, avoid:	**Titus 3:1** [a]Remind them [b]to be subject to rulers, to authorities, to be obedient, to be [c]ready for every good deed, **2** to malign no one, [a]to be peaceable, [a]gentle, [b]showing every consideration for all men. **3** [a]For we also once were foolish ourselves, [b]disobedient, [c]deceived, [d]enslaved to [e]various lusts and pleasures, spending our life in [f]malice and [f]envy, hateful, hating one another. **4** But when the [a]kindness of [b]God our Savior and *His* love for mankind [c]appeared, **5** [a]He saved us, [b]not on the basis of deeds which we have done in righteousness, but [c]according to His mercy, by the [d]washing of regeneration and [e]renewing by the Holy Spirit, **6** [a]whom He poured out upon us [b]richly through Jesus Christ our Savior, **7** so that being justified by His grace we would be made [a]heirs [1]according to *the* hope of eternal life. **8** [a]This is a trustworthy statement; and concerning these things I [b]want you to speak confidently, so that those who have [c]believed God will be careful to [d]engage in good deeds. These things are good and profitable for men. **9** But [a]avoid [b]foolish controversies and [c]genealogies and strife and [d]disputes about the Law, for they are [e]unprofitable and worthless. **10** [a]Reject a [b]factious man [c]after a first and second warning, **11** knowing that such a man is

for there is no profit in them, and they are vain. **10** An heretical man, after thou hast instructed him once and again, avoid: **11** and know thou, that such a man is perverse, and sinful, and self-condemned. **12** When I shall send Artemas to thee, or Tychicus, strive thou to come to me at Nicopolis; for I have purposed to winter there. **13** As for Zenas the scribe, and Apollos, endeavor to help them well on their way, that they may want nothing. **14** And let our people learn also to perform good works, on occasions of emergency, that they may not be unfruitful. **15** All they that are with me salute thee. Salute all them who love us in the faith. Grace be with you all. Amen.

*perverted and is sinning, being self-condemned.

Titus 3:12 When I send Artemas or *Tychicus to you, *make every effort to come to me at Nicopolis, for I have decided to *spend the winter there. **13** Diligently help Zenas the *lawyer and *Apollos on their way so that nothing is lacking for them. **14** *Our people must also learn to *engage in good 1deeds to meet *pressing needs, so that they will not be *unfruitful.

Titus 3:15 *All who are with me greet you. Greet those who love us *in *the* faith.

*Grace be with you all.

References to the New American Standard 1995

Titus 3:1
[a]2 Tim 2:14
[b]Rom 13:1
[c]2 Tim 2:21

Titus 3:2
[a]1 Tim 3:3; 1 Pet 2:18
[b]2 Tim 2:25

Titus 3:3
[a]Rom 11:30; Col 3:7
[b]Titus 1:16
[c]2 Tim 3:13
[d]Rom 6:6, 12
[e]2 Tim 3:6; Titus 2:12
[f]Rom 1:29

Titus 3:4
[a]Rom 2:4; Eph 2:7; 1 Pet 2:3
[b]Titus 2:10
[c]Titus 2:11

Titus 3:5
[a]Rom 11:14; 2 Tim 1:9
[b]Eph 2:9
[c]Eph 2:4; 1 Pet 1:3
[d]John 3:5; Eph 5:26; 1 Pet 3:21
[e]Rom 12:2

Titus 3:6
[a]Rom 5:5
[b]Rom 2:4; 1 Tim 6:17

Titus 3:7
[1]Or *of eternal life according to hope*
[a]Matt 25:34; Mark 10:17; Rom 8:17, 24; Titus 1:2

Titus 3:8
[a]1 Tim 1:15
[b]1 Tim 2:8
[c]2 Tim 1:12
[d]Titus 2:7, 14; 3:14

Titus 3:9
[a]2 Tim 2:16
[b]1 Tim 1:4; 2 Tim 2:23
[c]1 Tim 1:4
[d]James 4:1
[e]2 Tim 2:14

Titus 3:10
[a]2 John 10
[b]Rom 16:17
[c]Matt 18:15f

Titus 3:11
[a]Titus 1:14

Titus 3:12
[a]Acts 20:4; Eph 6:21f; Col 4:7f; 2 Tim 4:12
[b]2 Tim 4:9
[c]2 Tim 4:21

Titus 3:13
[a]Matt 22:35
[b]Acts 18:24; 1 Cor 16:12

Titus 3:14
[1]Or *occupations*
[a]Titus 2:8
[b]Titus 3:8
[c]Rom 12:13; Phil 4:16
[d]Matt 7:19; Phil 1:11; Col 1:10

Titus 3:15
[a]Acts 20:34
[b]1 Tim 1:2

ᶜCol 4:18

Koine Greek

Titus 3:1 Υπομιμνησκε αυτους αρχαις εξουσιαις υποτασσεσθαι, πειθαρχειν, προς παν εργον αγαθον ετοιμους ειναι, [2] μηδενα βλασφημειν, αμαχους ειναι, επιεικεις, πασαν ενδεικνυμενους πραυτητα προς παντας ανθρωπους. [3] Ημεν γαρ ποτε και ημεις ανοητοι, απειθεις, πλανωμενοι, δουλευοντες επιθυμιαις και ηδοναις ποικιλαις, εν κακια και φθονω διαγοντες, στυγητοι, μισουντες αλληλους.

Titus 3:4 οτε δε η χρηστοτης και η φιλανθρωπια επεφανη
του σωτηρος ημων θεου,
[5] ουκ εξ εργων των εν δικαιοσυνη
α εποιησαμεν ημεις
αλλα κατα το αυτου ελεος
εσωσεν ημας δια λουτρου παλιγγενεσιας
και ανακαινωσεως πνευματος αγιου,
[6] ου εξεχεεν εφ' ημας πλουσιως
δια Ιησου Χριστου του σωτηρος ημων,
[7] ινα δικαιωθεντες τη εκεινου χαριτι
κληρονομοι γενηθωμεν κατ' ελπιδα ζωης αιωνιου.

Titus 3:8 Πιστος ο λογος· και περι τουτων βουλομαι σε διαβεβαιουσθαι, ινα φροντιζωσιν καλων εργων προιστασθαι οι πεπιστευκοτες θεω· ταυτα εστιν καλα και ωφελιμα τοις ανθρωποις. [9] μωρας δε ζητησεις και γενεαλογιας και ερεις και μαχας νομικας περιιστασο· εισιν γαρ ανωφελεις και ματαιοι. [10] αιρετικον ανθρωπον μετα μιαν και δευτεραν νουθεσιαν παραιτου, [11] ειδως οτι εξεστραπται ο τοιουτος και αμαρτανει ων αυτοκατακριτος.

Titus 3:12 Οταν πεμψω Αρτεμαν προς σε η Τυχικον, σπουδασον ελθειν προς με εις Νικοπολιν, εκει γαρ κεκρικα παραχειμασαι. [13] Ζηναν τον νομικον και Απολλων σπουδαιως προπεμψον, ινα μηδεν αυτοις λειπη. [14] μανθανετωσαν δε και οι ημετεροι καλων εργων προιστασθαι εις τας αναγκαιας χρειας, ινα μη ωσιν ακαρποι.

Titus 3:15 Ασπαζονται σε οι μετ' εμου παντες. ασπασαι τους φιλουντας ημας εν πιστει.

Η χαρις μετα παντων υμων.

Language

  Process of Discovery

   Linguistics Section

    Linguistic Structure

[Definition of Godly living] 1 *a*Remind them *b*to be subject to rulers, to authorities, to be obedient, to be *c*ready for every good deed, **2** to malign no one, *a*to be peaceable, *a*gentle, *b*showing every consideration for all men. **3** *a*For we also once were foolish ourselves, *b*disobedient, *c*deceived, *d*enslaved to *e*various lusts and pleasures, spending our life in *f*malice and *f*envy, hateful, hating one another. **4** But when the *a*kindness of *b*God our Savior and *His* love for mankind *c*appeared, **5** *a*He saved us, *b*not on the basis of deeds which we have done in righteousness, but *c*according to His mercy, by the *d*washing of regeneration and *e*renewing by the Holy Spirit, **6** *a*whom He poured out upon us *b*richly through Jesus Christ our Savior, **7** so that being justified by His grace we would be made *a*heirs *1*according to *the* hope of eternal life. **8** *a*This is a trustworthy statement; and concerning these things I *b*want you to speak confidently, so that those who have *c*believed God will be careful to *d*engage in good deeds. These things are good and profitable for men. **9** But *a*avoid *b*foolish controversies and *c*genealogies and strife and *d*disputes about the Law, for they are *e*unprofitable and worthless. **10** *a*Reject a *b*factious man *c*after a first and second warning, **11** knowing that such a man is *a*perverted and is sinning, being self-condemned.

[Personal concerns] 12 When I send Artemas or *a*Tychicus to you, *b*make every effort to come to me at Nicopolis, for I have decided to *c*spend the winter there. **13** Diligently help Zenas the *a*lawyer and *b*Apollos on their way so that nothing is lacking for them. **14** *a*Our people must also learn to *b*engage in good *1*deeds to meet *c*pressing needs, so that they will not be *d*unfruitful.

[Good-bye] 15 *a*All who are with me greet you. Greet those who love us *b*in *the* faith. *c*Grace be with you all.

Discussion

This final chapter is a definition of what godly living must be. Paul concludes by offering the status of some of his companions.

Questioning the Passage

1. Why did Paul think all people were evil when they did not know Yeshua?

   The Apostle Paul, in his letters, often emphasized the sinful nature of all people, regardless of whether or not they knew Yeshua. This is a central theme in many of his writings, particularly in the book of Romans.

   Paul believed that all people, both Jews and Gentiles, were under the power of sin. In Romans 3:23, he writes, "for all have sinned and fall short of the glory of God." This includes those who did not know Yeshua. Paul's view was not that people were inherently evil, but rather that they were inherently sinful and in need of salvation.

   Paul also wrote about how trying to earn salvation through good works was not possible. In Romans 9:31-32, he says, "Because they did not seek it by faith, but as it were, by the works of the law. For they stumbled at that stumbling stone." This suggests that Paul saw those who did not know Yeshua as attempting to earn their way into Heaven through good works, which he viewed as futile.

   It's important to note that Paul's message was ultimately one of hope and redemption. He taught that while all have sinned, all can be justified freely by God's grace through the redemption that is in Yeshua (Romans 3:24). So, while Paul did recognize the sinful nature of humanity, he also emphasized the saving power of faith in Yeshua the Messiah.[9]

---

[9] 1. The complaints of Paul's Critics (11:6-12) - IVP new testament commentary series - bible gateway, accessed April 24, 2024, https://www.biblegateway.com/resources/ivp-nt/Complaints-Pauls-Critics.

2. What is the washing of new birth (regeneration)? (v. 5)

This is referring to baptism. It is believed when one is baptized in the name of Yeshua one gives up one's old life for the new life. This would be a regeneration of one's soul.

3. What does verse six mean?

This verse is part of a larger passage in Titus 3 that speaks about God's mercy and the regeneration and renewal brought about by the Holy Spirit.

The phrase "whom He poured out upon us richly" refers to the Holy Spirit. The Holy Spirit is given to believers in abundance, or "poured out richly," signifying the generous and abundant nature of God's grace.

The phrase "through Jesus Christ our Savior" indicates that this outpouring of the Holy Spirit comes through the mediation of Yeshua. It is through Yeshua's atonement and intercession that believers can receive the Holy Spirit.

This verse emphasizes the abundant outpouring of the Holy Spirit that believers receive through Yeshua. It underscores the richness of God's mercy and the transformative power of the Holy Spirit in the life of a believer.[10]

4. Is eternal life guaranteed in verse seven?

Eternal life is a hope that all Christians have. The author reminds the readers that Yeshua gave his life not only for the forgiveness of our sins but also for the hope of eternal life.

---

[10] 1. Titus 3:6 Commentaries: whom He poured out upon us richly through Jesus Christ our Savior, accessed April 24, 2024, https://biblehub.com/commentaries/titus/3-6.htm.

5. Why does verse eight talks about good deeds when verse five says that our good deeds do not give justification?

   A conflict the church had in those days and still today is that good deeds do not automatically give you justification. That means you do not get to be automatically saved by Yeshua because you did good things. Justification, forgiveness of sin, is a gift that God gives us freely. However, the church had to deal with the problem that once you had justification, you needed to do good things. Just because Yeshua died for your sin does not mean that you are allowed to go out and sin.

6. What are the pressing needs or emergencies in verse fourteen?

   According to the author, pressing needs were the things that were needed to be done to ensure that the community stayed in the expression of Christianity that Paul believed was the only expression of Christianity.

Biblical Personalities

1. Artemas - Unfortunately, not much is known about Artemas from other biblical texts. However, in Titus 3:12, Paul indicated he planned to send Artemas to Crete. Artemas was likely a faithful and capable teacher, and Paul considered him suitable to replace Titus in his ministry there. Tradition suggests that Artemas later became the Bishop of Lystra.

2. Tychicus - Tychicus appears in several New Testament writings. He was a close friend and trusted assistant of Paul. In Acts 20:4, Colossians 4:7, 2 Timothy 4:12, and Titus 3:12, Tychicus is mentioned. Paul describes him as a beloved brother

and a faithful minister. Tychicus was entrusted with important missions to distant churches, highlighting his significance in Paul's eyes. In Titus 3:12, Paul instructs Titus to be diligent in coming to him when he sends either Artemas or Tychicus. Tychicus was likely one of Paul's most esteemed companions[1].

3. Zenas – He played a role in early Christian ministry, and his expertise in the law likely contributed to his significance in Paul's instructions to Titus.

4. Apollos - He is known from various New Testament passages. He was an Alexandrian scholar who had a deep understanding of the Scriptures. Initially, he was catechized by Aquila and Priscilla in the ways of the Lord. Apollos was a disciple of John the Baptist and later converted to Christianity. His eloquence and knowledge made him a prominent teacher.

   o Acts 18: Apollos is mentioned in Acts 18:24-28. He was fervent in spirit and taught accurately about Jesus, although he only knew the baptism of John. Aquila and Priscilla took him aside and explained the way of God more accurately.
   o 1 Corinthians 1: In 1 Corinthians 1:12, some Corinthians identified themselves as followers of Apollos.
   o 1 Corinthians 3: Paul addresses divisions among the Corinthians, mentioning Apollos as one of the teachers they were following.
   o 1 Corinthians 16: Paul planned to send Apollos to visit the Corinthian community again, but Apollos was reluctant to go (1 Corinthians 16:1).
   o Acts 19: Apollos is also mentioned in Acts 19:1, where he traveled to Ephesus.

- o Friend of Paul: Apollos became a close friend and associate of St. Paul. Although he had the potential to rival or even supersede Paul's authority over the churches along the Mediterranean coast, Apollos chose to remain loyal and devoted to Paul. Paul treated him as an equal power in the Church of Christ, alongside St. Peter.

- o Authorship of Hebrews: Martin Luther suggested that Apollos might be the unknown writer of the Epistle to the Hebrews. However, this remains a debated point, and the authorship of Hebrews has been disputed since the days of Origen in the third century.

- o Name Origin: It's interesting to note that the names of these three friends of St. Paul—Zenas, Artemas, and Apollos—were derived from three famous heathen deities: Zenas from Zeus, Artemas from Artemis, and Apollos from the well-known sun-god.

In summary, Apollos played a significant role in early Christian ministry, and his eloquence and knowledge made him a respected teacher and friend of Paul.

Biblical Locations

1. Nicopolis

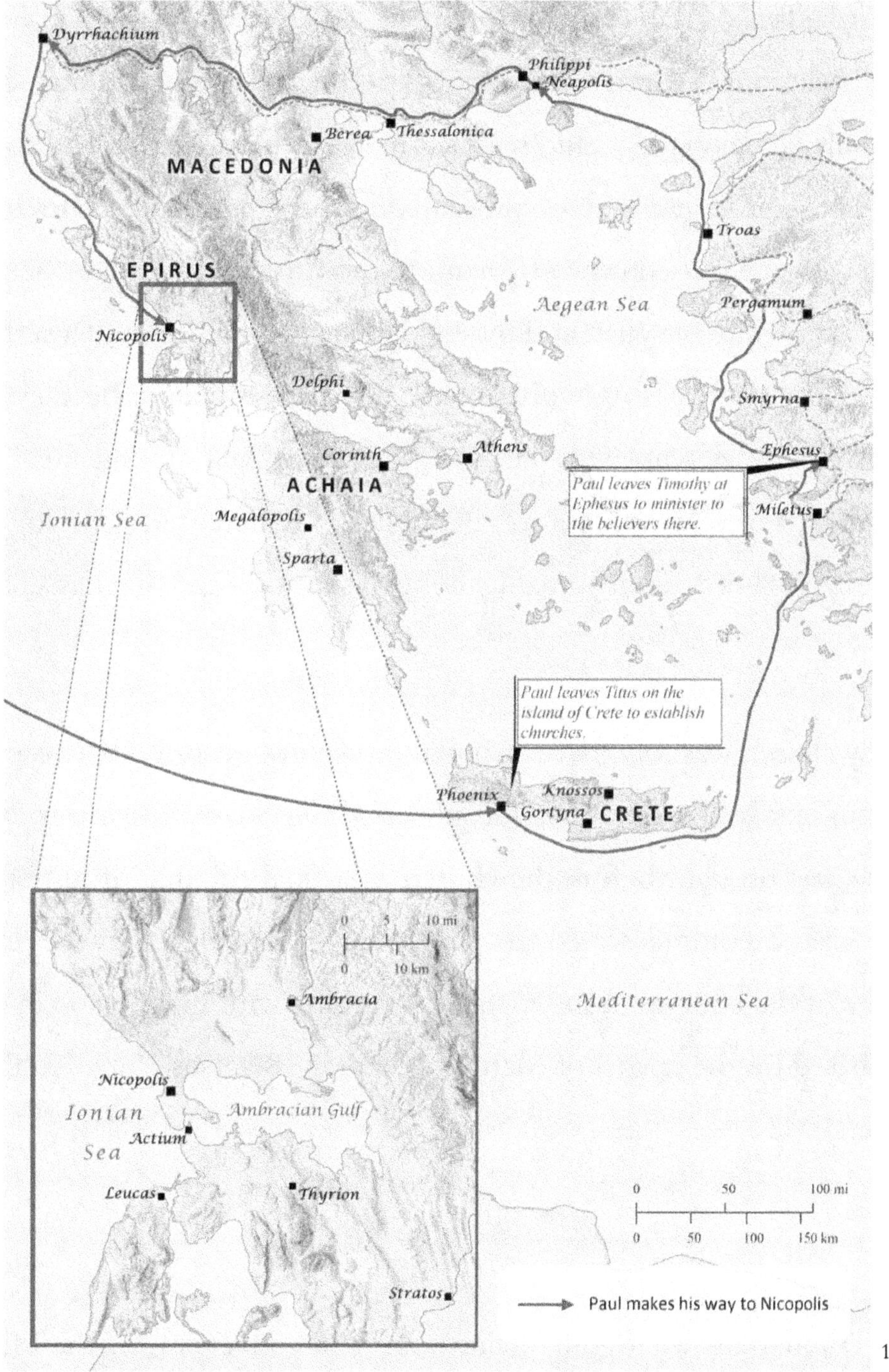

11

---

[11] 1. Posted byAdministrator, "Nicopolis and Its Surroundings," Bible Mapper Atlas, April 18, 2024, https://biblemapper.com/blog/index.php/2023/01/02/nicopolis-and-its-surroundings/.

Culture Section

Discussion

In the early days of the Yeshua movement, little was known about his genealogy and his background. Disagreements occurred even within Christian circles about what family he belonged to and whether he was truly a descendent of King David or not. The genealogies that are presented in the Gospels are controversial. They would have been passed down by hand to mouth and could have been corrupted over the years. The Assyrian and the Babylonian captivities dealt a serious blow to Israel's genealogies. Many people could not prove what tribe they were from, especially the Jews who were taken captive and lived among the Gentiles and pagans for many years. Therefore, Paul might say here that genealogy is not that important. Yeshua offered humanity hope of salvation and that has all that matters.

The early church was told that when major disputes occurred between people that the parties involved should seek the advice of the elders. When this did not work, the issue was brought before the church as a final tribunal of justice. The guilty person was excommunicated or temporarily ousted from the church. The members of the congregation would stop dealing with that person in all manners. This is based on the gospel of Matthew chapter 18 verses 15 to 18. This is meant by verse 10.

Thoughts

This letter emphasizes what godly living was. The conversion of the Mithras house churches into Yeshua house churches went well for Paul. However, there were accepted behaviors that the people did under the cult that were not acceptable to Paul. He wanted a pure version of Yeshua worship. In his expression of Christianity, a lot of Semitic behaviors were incorporated. This set the new Christian religion apart from the old Mithras Cult religion.

Bibliography

byAdministrator, Posted. "Nicopolis and Its Surroundings." Bible Mapper Atlas, April 18, 2024. https://biblemapper.com/blog/index.php/2023/01/02/nicopolis-and-its-surroundings/.

The complaints of Paul's Critics (11:6-12) - IVP new testament commentary series - bible gateway. Accessed April 24, 2024. https://www.biblegateway.com/resources/ivp-nt/Complaints-Pauls-Critics.

Gordon, Ronald J. Apostle Paul and the winds of crete, February 18, 2016. https://cob-net.org/compare_crete.php.

GotQuestions.org. "Home." GotQuestions.org, April 26, 2016. https://www.gotquestions.org/ungodly-ungodliness.html.

Paul VargasPaul Vargas 3, Steve can help♦Steve can help 5, JosephJoseph 16.7k11 gold badge3636 silver badges9494 bronze badges, DrFryDrFry 1, Ozzie OzzieOzzie Ozzie 13.8k44 gold badges4242 silver badges8383 bronze badges, Walter SWalter S 85811 gold badge55 silver badges88 bronze badges, and Mario GMario G 711 bronze badge. "What Does Paul Mean by 'Sound Doctrine' in Titus 2:1." Biblical Hermeneutics Stack Exchange, January 1, 1960. https://hermeneutics.stackexchange.com/questions/8649/what-does-paul-mean-by-sound-doctrine-in-titus-21.

Titus 3:6 Commentaries: whom He poured out upon us richly through Jesus Christ our Savior,. Accessed April 24, 2024. https://biblehub.com/commentaries/titus/3-6.htm.

West, Posted by Marsha, and Marsha West. "What Is Sound Doctrine?" Christian Research Network, February 15, 2017. https://christianresearchnetwork.org/2017/02/15/what-is-sound-doctrine/.

"What Is Sound Doctrine?" Ligonier Ministries. Accessed April 15, 2024. https://www.ligonier.org/learn/articles/what-sound-doctrine.